First World War
and Army of Occupation
War Diary
France, Belgium and Germany

36 DIVISION
107 Infantry Brigade,
Brigade Trench Mortar Battery
26 September 1915 - 31 August 1916

WO95/2503/7

The Naval & Military Press Ltd
www.nmarchive.com
Published in association with The National Archives

Published by

The Naval & Military Press Ltd

Unit 10 Ridgewood Industrial Park,

Uckfield, East Sussex,

TN22 5QE England

Tel: +44 (0) 1825 749494

www.naval-military-press.com

www.nmarchive.com

This diary has been reprinted in facsimile from the original. Any imperfections are inevitably reproduced and the quality may fall short of modern type and cartographic standards.

© **Crown Copyright**
Images reproduced by permission of The National Archives, London, England, 2015.

Contents

Document type	Place/Title	Date From	Date To
Heading	WO95/2503/7 Brigade Trench Mortar Battery		
Heading	36th Division 107th Infy Bde 107th Trench Mortar Bty. Jly-Aug 1916 (Oct-Nov 1915 93 Tab)		
Miscellaneous	3rd Army 67 Bde 107 Bde 36 Div 36 Div 94th Trench Mortar Batty Vol I Oct 15		
War Diary		26/09/1915	25/10/1915
Heading	94 Trench Mortar Batty Nov 1915 Vol II		
War Diary	St Omer	03/11/1915	31/07/1916
Heading	War Diary Of The 107th Trench Mortar Battery From 1st August 1916 To 31st August 1916 Volume II		
War Diary	Opposite Messines	01/08/1916	31/08/1916

WO95/2503/7

Brigade Trench Mortar Battery

36TH DIVISION
107TH INFY BDE

107TH TRENCH MORTAR BTY.

JLY - AUG 1916

(OCT - NOV 1915 93 TMB)

3rd Army

67 RL. 2/2
121/7384
107 BDE 36 DIV
Attendant 36 DIV

9th Trench Mortar Batty.
Vol I
Oct 15

31.10.15.

War Diary.

94th Trench Mortar Battery.

Sept. 26th 1915. Attached to 67th Inf. Brigade, 22nd Division. Stationed at Framerville.

Oct. 17th 7.30 p.m. Fired 11 rounds on German trenches round two edges of Bois Etoilé. 4 blinds. Enemy observed next morning repairing trenches.
A few of the rounds were fired at communication trenches in the wood. Impossible to observe precise result.

Oct. 19th. Fired two rounds 3 p.m. at German observing or sniper's post. Both blinds.

Oct. 20th. 6.30. a.m. Fired seven rounds at enemy trenches. 2 blinds.

Oct. 25th. Battery attached to 107th Inf. Bde, 36th Division. Stationed at St. Ouen, Somme.

R. Denne. 2Lt.

O.C. 94th Trench Mortar Battery.

GHG 4
107 Bala 121/7637

9A Irenean Motion Bay
Nov 19, 15

Vol II

Army Form C. 2118

WAR DIARY
or
INTELLIGENCE SUMMARY

94th Trench Mortar Battery

(Erase heading not required.)

Instructions regarding War Diaries and Intelligence Summaries are contained in F.S. Regs., Part II. and the Staff Manual respectively. Title Pages will be prepared in manuscript.

Place	Date	Hour	Summary of Events and Information	Remarks and references to Appendices
St Ouen	3/11/15		Marched with 107th Inf Bde to Mailly-Maillet, where attached to 4th Division.	
	22.11.15	3.30 p.m.	Fired three rounds in retaliation to minenwerfer. Enemy's gun silenced. 1 blind.	
	24.11.15	9 a.m.	Fired nine rounds in retaliation to German mortars. Considerable damage to enemy trenches. 1 dug-out blown up. 2 blinds. Ammunition on the whole satisfactory.	

R. Deane 2Lt.
O.C. 94th T.M.By.
30.11.15.

36th Division
107th Trench Mortar Battery

WAR DIARY or INTELLIGENCE SUMMARY

Army Form 3 July 1916 107 T.M.B.

Vol I

Place	Date	Hour	Summary of Events and Information	Remarks and references to Appendices
	July 1st	7.30am	2nd Lieut Thorpe and 25 men under 2nd Lieut Thorpe joined the 10th R.I. Rifles in AVELUY WOOD and moved up with the Battn. carrying 50 bombs. After crossing River Ancre the rear half company of 10 R.I.R. was held up by machine gun & trench mortar fire from THIEPVAL VILLAGE. Lieut Thorpe with 2 N.C.Os went forward apparently to try and get them on but Lt Thorpe and one of the N.C.Os fell wounded. These guns did not get out of the wood and one was knocked out. Lieut Lloyd, Dodd and 75 O.R. took 2 mortars & 50 bombs from the 9th R.I. Rifles and marched up behind the Battn. to the top of AVELUY WOOD, there however owing to the confusion of wounded and German prisoners coming back the section got split in two & lost touch. Lieut Lloyd Dead and some of the section pushed on and eventually joined up with Lt Browns section the guns were brought into action near OMAGH (G9) where they rendered great assistance in breaking up the German	

WAR DIARY or INTELLIGENCE SUMMARY

Army Form C. 2118.

counter attack. After expending all his bombs, Lt Lloyd both withdrew his guns to 'A' line and on general retirement they were brought back to GORDON CASTLE to my Hd. Qrs. One section of 2 guns with 25 men carrying 50 bombs under Lieut J.B. Brown joined the 8th Rl Rifles in AVELUY WOOD and made up behind the Batn. On the advance Lieut Brown was wounded but Sergt Brown kept the section together, they eventually joined us with Lieut Lloyd and at OMA G H (B9). From the information I have received it appears evident that owing to the heavy weights being carried the men arrived at the top of THIEPVAL WOOD in an exhausted condition which made the task of keeping together and in touch with the Battalions almost impossible in the congestion of wounded & prisoners. I should like to bring to notice the able handling of Sergt Brown.

Army Form C. 2118.

WAR DIARY
or
INTELLIGENCE SUMMARY

(Erase heading not required.)

Instructions regarding War Diaries and Intelligence Summaries are contained in F. S. Regs., Part II. and the Staff Manual respectively. Title Pages will be prepared in manuscript.

Place	Date	Hour	Summary of Events and Information	Remarks and references to Appendices
	July 1st		Three guns were lost during the operations but same were found in the wood to replace them.	
	2-7-16	3pm	Moved out of trenches to Martinsart.	
	3-7-16		Billets	
	4-7-16		Moved to Senlis ville	
	5-7-16		Moved to Puchevillers - Paradis	
	6-7-16		" "	
	7-7-16			
	8-7-16			
	9-7-16			
	10-7-16		Moved to Bernaville.	
	11-7-16		Marched to Auxi Le Chateau and entrained for Thiennes arrived 11/30pm then marched to Wardrecques arrived 4-30 12/7/16.	
	13-7-16	7.30am	March to Mont Lenlinghem.	

2449 Wt. W14957/Mgo 750,000 1/16 J.B.C. & A. Forms/C.2118/12.

Army Form C. 2118.

WAR DIARY
or
INTELLIGENCE SUMMARY
(Erase heading not required.)

Place	Date	Hour	Summary of Events and Information	Remarks and references to Appendices
	14-7-16		Parades.	
	15-7-16		"	
	16-7-16		"	
	17-7-16		"	
	18-7		"	
	19-7		"	
	20-7-16		Moved to Bollezeele.	
	21-7-16		Moved to Rosendael.	
	22-7-16		Moved to Ly Marie Cappel.	
	23-7-16		Moved to Steenvoord.	
	24-7-16		Parades	
	25-7-16		"	
	26-7		"	
	27-7		"	
	28-7-16		Moved to Kortepyp	
	29-7		Parades	
	30-7		"	
	31-7		Relieved 108th Trench in trenches	

H/Stewart Loos 107th Trench Mortar Battery

Vol 2

Confidential

War Diary

of

The 107th Trench Mortar Battery

from 1st August 1916 to 31st August 1916

Volume II

WAR DIARY
~~INTELLIGENCE SUMMARY~~

(Erase heading not required.)

Army Form C. 2118.

Place	Date	Hour	Summary of Events and Information	Remarks and references to Appendices
Opposite MESSINES	1-8-16 to 5-8-16		During this period the Battery remained in the trenches where they had relieved the 108th TRENCH MORTAR BATTERY on the 31st July. There were two emplacements in this sector, one near the front line opposite LA PETITE DOUVE FARM (U.8.a.3.0), + one in "THE LOOP" near Boyle's Farm (T.6.b. 98.30). One gun was kept in each emplacement during the day; they were brought back into reserve emplacements during the night, where they were held in readiness to fire on our own front line in case of need. A few rounds were fired each day from LA PETITE DOUVE emplacement in retaliation to enemy trench mortars. The total for the period amounted to 38	References to Trench Map, Sheet 28 S.W. ppm
"	5-8-16	4 p.m. (about)	On this day, the 108th TRENCH MORTAR BTY. took over the emplacement at LA PETITE DOUVE. The 107th Battery took over four one gun emplacements from the TRENCH MORTAR BATTERY, + the emplacement at "THE LOOP". 14 9th TRENCH MORTAR BATTERY, + the emplacement at "THE LOOP". These five guns being retained, this made a total of 5 guns in the line. During the relief, Lieutenant over the German trenches from ONTARIO FM. to the WYTSCHAETE-WULVERGEM road, at ranges ranging from 250 yds to 400 yds. During the relief, Lieutenant J.J. Stewart was slightly wounded, + subsequently proceeded to hospital. This left only one officer, Lieut P.S. Murray, to any gun in the new sector. The emplacements are in the following positions:- No.1, in trench off DURHAM ROAD	ppm

WAR DIARY
or
INTELLIGENCE SUMMARY

(Erase heading not required.)

Army Form C. 2118.

Date	Hour	Summary of Events and Information	Remarks and references to Appendices
7-8-16	3¼ p.m. to 6 p.m.	TRENCH in D3 sector (N.36.c.8.8.); No.2 in "GROUSE BUTT" (N.36.c.6.5), No 3 in front line at N.36.d.2.2.; No 4 in front line at T.6.b.3.6., & No 5, as already described, at THE LOOP near BOYLES' FARM (T.6.b.98.2.9).	P/sen
8th	6 p.m. each day	114 rounds were fired in retaliation to enemy mortars	P/sen
		104 rounds were fired in retaliation. 2nd Lt Gray having reported for duty, proceeded to the trenches to assist Capt. Murray, & took charge of No. 4 & 5 guns.	P/sen
9th	4 p.m.	70 rounds were fired in retaliation. Lieut Stewart has returned from hospital.	P/sen
10th	10 a.m.	The men in the trenches were relieved by the men who had been resting at KORTE PYP. Capt. Murray & Lt Gray were relieved by Lieut Stewart now & 2nd Lt Hollowhead	P/sen
	3.4 p.m.	224 rounds were fired in retaliation	##
11th	4 p.m. to 5 p.m.	44 rounds fired	P/sen
		The re-building of No 2 emplacement at GROUSE-BUTTS was commenced, with the assistance of the ROYAL ENGINEERS.	
12th	4 p.m.	The enemy started his usual bombardment. We replied by firing 52 rounds out of our front & support lines.	P/sen
	5.30 p.m.	In conjunction with the 2 in. mortars we fired 76 additional rounds	P/sen

WAR DIARY
or
INTELLIGENCE SUMMARY

(Erase heading not required.)

Army Form C. 2118.

Place	Date	Hour	Summary of Events and Information	Remarks and references to Appendices
	13·8·16		Possibly because it was Sunday, the enemy did not start his usual bombardment at 4 o'clock or thereabouts. After waiting for him for some time, we opened ourselves in sympathy with the 2 in. mortars at	Pfrm
		4.50 a.m.	4.50 a.m. 97 aerotabs were fired. It was thought that a direct hit was obtained on a trench-mortar emplacement N. of ONTARIO F^m Enemy's reply was feeble.	
	14·8·16		It was decided to make a new emplacement at BOYLE'S FARM, the present one in THE LOOP being too exposed. Excavation was accordingly commenced. There were no rounds fired today by either side.	Pfrm
	15·8·16	10.30 a.m.	Relief was carried out. Relieving party were under the command of 2nd Lieut J.T. Stevenson & 2nd Lieut A.M.Gray. No firing.	Pfrm
	16·8·16	3 p.m.	2nd Lieut A.M.Gray & one Rifleman were killed by a shell hitting the parapet in front line in front of No 5 emplacement.	P.M.
		4 p.m.	The enemy in reply to a bombardment by the 19th Division on our left,	

WAR DIARY
or
INTELLIGENCE SUMMARY

(Erase heading not required.)

Army Form C. 2118.

Place	Date	Hour	Summary of Events and Information	Remarks and references to Appendices
	17.8.16		bombarded our trenches in the vicinity of Nos 1, 2 & 3 emplacements. We replied, firing 107 rounds. There was very little action on the right. It is worth noting that while no damage was done on the left, where there was a heavy bombardment, almost the only shot fired during the day in the vicinity of No 5 gun caused two casualties. Capt Murray proceeded to the trenches to take the place of 2nd Lt Gray. All quiet & no firing	P.S.M. P.S.M. B.S.M.
	18.8.16		No firing	
	19.8.16	3.25 p.m.	(25m) 83 rounds fired in retaliation; action lasted 20 minutes. No 3 gun got into enemy's emplacement	A.M.
	20.8.16	16.20 a.m.	Relief carried out. No firing. One Rifleman received a bullet wound in the arm, thought to be self-inflicted. He was standing in front of No 1 gun at the time.	
	21.8.16	4 p.m.	101 rounds fired in retaliation by Nos 1, 3, & 4 guns. No mortars on the right. It is 11 days since the enemy minenwerfer at ONTARIO FM. has been active. Possibly the direct hit obtained on 13th inst had good effect	F.S.M.

Army Form C. 2118.

WAR DIARY
or
INTELLIGENCE SUMMARY
(Erase heading not required.)

Place	Date	Hour	Summary of Events and Information	Remarks and references to Appendices
	22-8-16	6.45 a.m.	Enemy did not open till 6.45 p.m. — much later than usual. 34 rounds fired in reply. Still quiet at No 5 emplacement	P.F.m
	23-8-16		2nd Lt Hollinshead went to hospital with fever. No firing	P.F.m
	24-8-16		84 rounds fired	P.F.m
	25-8-16		Relief carried out. No firing	P.F.m
	26-8-16		The first layer of cement was placed on the roof of the No 2 emplacement today. 2 Other Ranks went sick & were admitted to hospital. No firing. One Other Rank admitted to hospital (sick)	P.F.m
	27-8-16		Early in the morning the front sentry in front of No 4 gun was blown in. It became necessary to move the gun to a temporary emplacement 100 yards to the right. No firing.	P.F.m
	28-8-16		98 rounds fired. One O.R. admitted to hospital (sick)	P.F.m

WAR DIARY
or
INTELLIGENCE SUMMARY

Army Form C. 2118.

Place	Date	Hour	Summary of Events and Information	Remarks and references to Appendices
	29.8.16		No trench mortar activity on either side today.	B/um
			Guns were kept in the front line emplacements tonight in anticipation of gas attack from our trenches. Intention was to fire 280 rounds in conjunction with artillery.	
		10 P.M.	Received message that attack was postponed & withdrew guns to defence positions.	B/um
	30.8.16	2 P.M.	19th Division Trench Mortars registered on enemy lines. Germans retaliated. Some of their mortars falling in our area (D2). We fired 5·5" rounds from our Nos. 3 & 5" gun, with good effect.	B/um
		3 P.M.	Our Heavy gun fired 4 rounds in answer to German rifle-grenades. Guns went in tonight, as we were informed that a gas attack was cancelled, and withdrew all guns except No 1 (Heavy).	
	31.8.16	1 A.M.	We were informed that gas attack was cancelled, and withdrew all guns except No 1 (Heavy). This gun was not informed of postponement.	B/um
		11·34 A.M.	Our artillery started their bombardment. We turned up No. 5" gun & fired 28 rounds before w/o. No. 1 fired 54 gun were then withdrawn.	
		3·15 P.M.	Strafe which began in 19th Division area spread to our area to the enemy put out a S.O.S large mortars. We replied with 36 & T.C. stopped firing. Our trench gun put over 12 rounds in answer to German rifle-grenades.	

Army Form C. 2118.